OUR HIDDEN

Beverley Birch

Photograp

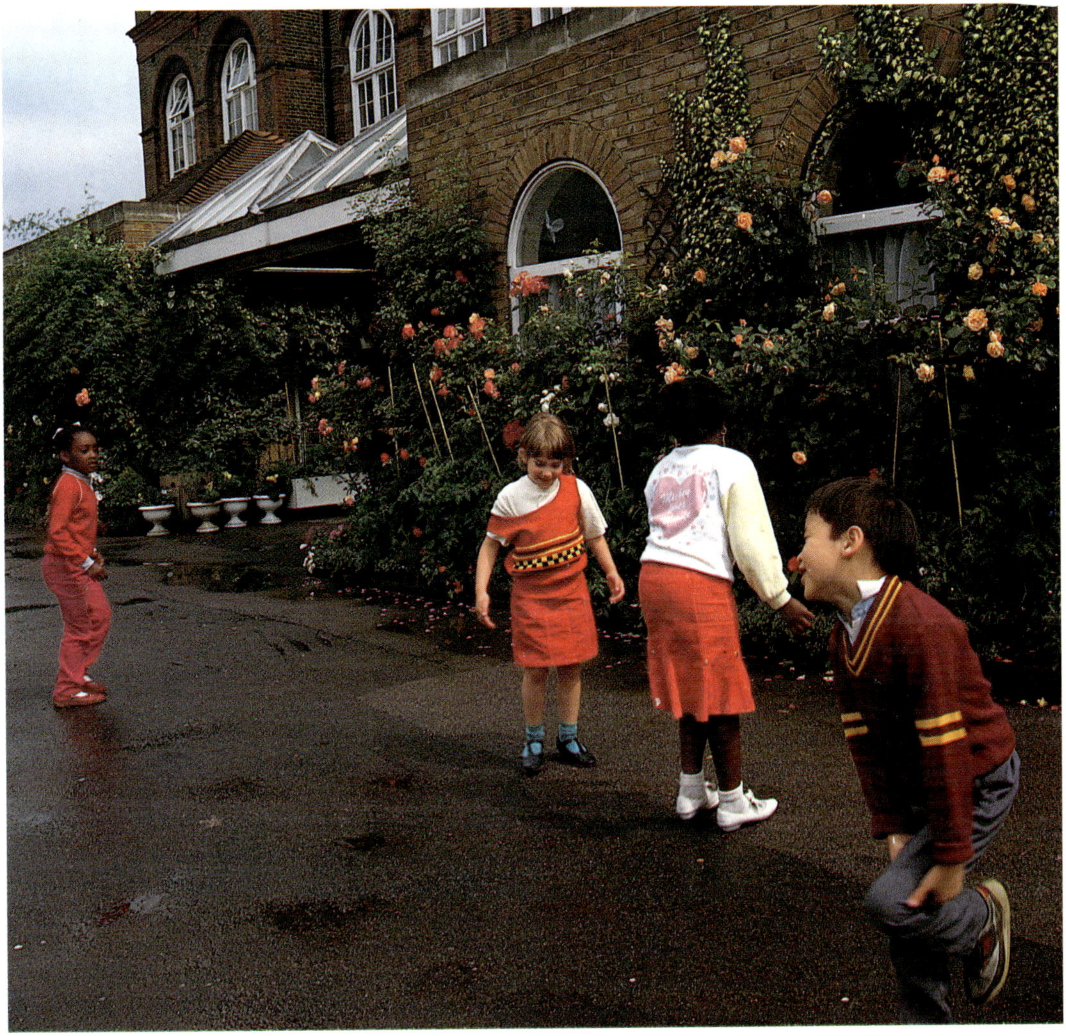

Hamish Hamilton London

Our school is on a big, long, noisy road. There aren't many parks nearby, only lorries, cars, shops and a lot of brick walls.

There used to be some trees along the road but a hurricane blew quite a few of them down. And there aren't even any gardens to look at as you walk along the pavement. In winter it can be quite bleak.

But when we turn through our school gate, everything is bright with trees, flowers and climbing plants. This is our hidden garden.

Our garden is our playground. And our playground is our garden. We grow flowers, trees, fruit and vegetables here. Suzi likes climbing as high as she can to look at it all. Kate thinks it looks better upside down.

The plants are growing well this year. That's because we have looked after the garden carefully. We start growing seeds in the classroom early in the spring when it is still cold outside. We keep them warm and damp.

'Nothing's happening yet,' says Nicolette. She checks the pots every day. Then one morning there's a tiny green shoot pushing up through the soil. Then more and more, and the first leaves uncurling.

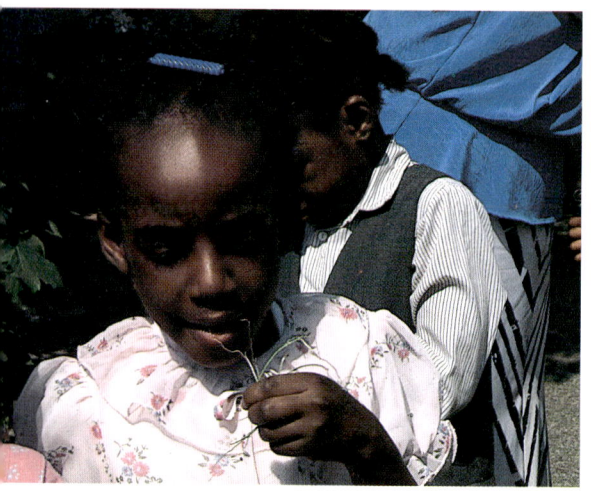

As soon as the weather is warm enough, we can start planting them out in the garden. Some of the seedlings are still very tiny. Ferrone has a spring onion, and she holds on to it very tightly. She's worried that it might blow away.

'I know the best place to put our plants,' Kodi tells Buke. She has already picked a patch in the sunniest part of the flower bed.

All through the spring and summer, there are things to be done in the garden. Kate and Zeenat start weeding and clearing up dead leaves and twigs.

Binh prefers hunting for insect pests that might eat the plants. Last year all our runner beans vanished overnight. We never found out what ate them.

The birds have been making a feast of our cherries. We have made a scarecrow to stand guard for us. 'Let's put him here,' says Leah, trying to make him stand upright. 'That should scare them off.'

'Make sure you only take out the dead leaves and twigs.
Don't take any young plants,' Anne Marie reminds Kate.
Kate is more interested in the spiders. She just saw one
scuttle away among the flowers.

Binh is smelling the roses. Their scent is so strong that it drifts into the classrooms in the afternoons.

'Yuk,' says Anne Marie. 'What's that?'
'It's only a slug,' says Kate, but chases her anyway.

Because the garden is looking so good this year, we decide to have a garden picnic to celebrate.

It's still early summer and most of our fruit isn't ripe yet, so we make a trip to the market. Akhlak picks out a good bunch of bananas.

'Let's have some peaches too,' says Angela, who has reached the front of the queue. 'And some oranges and apples, then we can make a really big fruit salad.'

Suzi and Xuong are more interested in the chopping and slicing and mixing.
'I'm going to eat some of this,' says Suzi.
'Not till the picnic, I hope,' Xuong tells her.

Everyone gets busy preparing sandwiches and salads, cakes and biscuits.

The scarecrow has kept the birds off the cherries, and there is quite a good crop now. They're ripe enough to make a cherry pie for our picnic. 'And some cherry tarts,' insists Anne Marie.

'It's very tiring taking out all these stones,' complains Leah.
'Make sure you do,' says Zeenat.
'I don't want to break my teeth!'

'Are you sure that's right, Kate?' asks Binh, very doubtfully. 'I think *I'd* better put the sugar in.'

Suddenly the weather begins to change. It starts to get very dark, with a strong wind blowing.

'Just our luck! It's going to rain,' says Anne Marie gloomily. She's right. Within minutes it is pouring. That finishes any hope of our picnic outdoors.

But we've prepared so much food! It seems a pity not to eat it. Well, we could have an inside picnic, and look at the garden through the rain!

For a while everyone is in a flurry, arranging the food on tables in the school hall. But when all the plates and dishes are laid out, it's well worth the trouble.

There is some disagreement about who's going to have the first bite of cherry tart.

15

After the picnic, of course, the rain stops! There's even a bit of watery sun, and it's nice to be out in the garden again.

We skip to see who can keep going the longest. Anne Marie seems to be able to go on and on. Binh gets fed up with the skipping. He's got other plans for his rope, though he won't tell anyone what they are.

It's getting so warm that we can take our work outside for the whole afternoon.
'Is "cherry pie" one word or two?' wonders Leah.

The weather gets better and better. It's a good thing, because some of the fruit in the garden is ready for harvesting, and we have to start tidying up for the winter. No one likes gardening in the pouring rain!

It's one of the best apple crops we've had in years. The apples are big and very juicy.

'We ought to have a peach tree,' says Kate. 'We ought to try and grow one.'
'We could all eat a peach and grow the stones,' suggests Zeenat, looking hungrily at the apple. 'We might get a forest!'

The scarecrow has been really useful this year. He kept the birds off the tomatoes and they're ripening fast. We decide to pick them all in case there is any more rain.

'There are enough here to make tomato soup,' says Wai Kuen,
who is in charge of the basket and can feel it getting heavy.

'Darren's crying,' says Louisa, feeling sorry for him.
'It's the onions,' Darren sobs.

Even though the tomatoes and onions have been cooked, it's quite hard work pushing them all through the sieve. Toyin and Louisa take turns for a while, until all the juice is in the bowl.

'I hope there's going to be enough soup for me,' says Louisa.

It really is quite delicious, and it tastes all the better because we grew the tomatoes and made the soup ourselves.

The days get colder and colder. Winter is here. The fruit trees and the flower beds are all bare, and most of the colours have gone.

But the climbers already have tiny buds on them, and the tips of daffodils are poking through the soil. It won't be long before it is spring again, and then our garden will bloom once more.

HAMISH HAMILTON CHILDREN'S BOOKS

Published by the Penguin Group
27 Wrights Lane, London W8 5TZ, England
Viking Penguin Inc., 40 West 23rd Street, New York, New York 10010, U.S.A.
Penguin Books Australia Ltd, Ringwood, Victoria, Australia
Penguin Books Canada Ltd, 2801 John Street, Markham, Ontario, Canada L3R 1B4
Penguin Books (N.Z.) Ltd, 182-190 Wairau Road, Auckland 10, New Zealand

Penguin Books Ltd, Registered Offices: Harmondsworth, Middlesex, England

First published in Great Britain 1988 by
Hamish Hamilton Children's Books

Design by Tony Garret

British Library Cataloguing in Publication Data

Birch, Beverley
Our hidden garden.
I. Inner London. Multicultural education
I. Title   II. Series
370.11'5

ISBN 0-241-12519-7

Printed in Singapore